LET'S GO WA

Twelve short circular walks arou
the less able and families wiu ﹍

Enjoy!

[signature]

Front cover picture: Barnwell Church

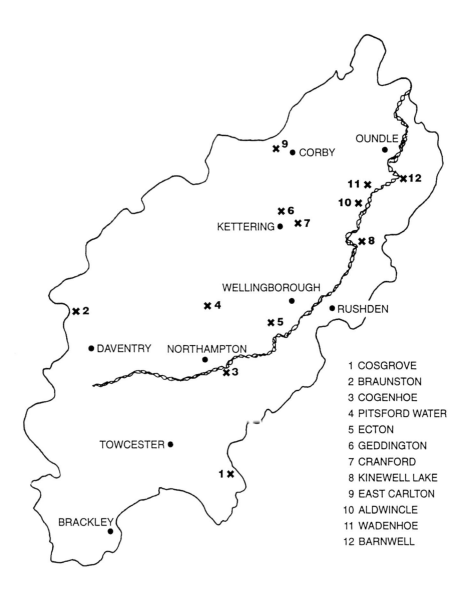

OUNDLE

×9 ● CORBY

11 **×**   **×12**

10 **×**

×6

KETTERING ● **×7**

WELLINGBOROUGH

×2   **×4**   ● RUSHDEN

×5

● DAVENTRY   NORTHAMPTON

×3

1 COSGROVE
2 BRAUNSTON
3 COGENHOE
4 PITSFORD WATER
5 ECTON
TOWCESTER ●   6 GEDDINGTON
7 CRANFORD
1 **×**   8 KINEWELL LAKE
9 EAST CARLTON
10 ALDWINCLE
BRACKLEY ●   11 WADENHOE
12 BARNWELL

×8

LET'S GO WALKABOUT!
IN NORTHAMPTONSHIRE

Walks for the less agile

Mia Butler

W. D. WHARTON
Wellingborough

First published in 1996 by
W.D. Wharton
37 Sheep Street
Wellingborough
Northamptonshire NN8 1BX

ISBN 1 899597 02 6

Designed and typeset by John Hardaker
Wollaston, Northamptonshire
Printed and bound in Great Britain by
Stanley L. Hunt (Printers) Ltd., Midland Road, Rushden

Contents

Acknowledgements

To Jane Draper who drew the maps, Bill Dalton, Colin Eaton and Marian Pipe who took the photos, and all who assisted and encouraged me as I hobbled round the countryside on two walking sticks to prove that it could be done – and for the fortifying cups of tea en route – thank you.

Introduction

The suggested walks in this book are specially picked for those whose spirit is willing but whose flesh is weak, yet who are nevertheless eager to get out and explore new horizons. The walks are, for the most part, circular – bringing you back to your start point with the minimum of backtracking – and some of them are suitable for wheelchairs, or families with small children (in or out of pushchairs), such as the village circuit at Geddington. Each itinerary includes reference to details such as stiles, gates and slopes, and all the walks have been tried and tested (by one with an impediment!), but changeable local conditions, such as overgrown foliage or winter floods, must be taken into account.

Many of the county's hamlets and villages are enchanting in themselves and should not be dismissed when considering quiet country walks. A wealth of charm exists in the old thatch cottages and lovingly tended gardens and arbours, which cannot but delight the eye. Ancient churches, and many a sage saying etched on the weathered headstones in their churchyards, provide insight to our distant past, and the motley variety of lichens, wildflowers and, indeed, wildlife reflect an oasis of serenity.

Look, too, for our 'castle sites', steeped in the history of our warring ancestors, and for the romance of local myths and legends which abound in our county, where almost every community boasts a ghost! Heritage Sites, too, can yield a mass of information, and often exist in unexpected places. Dovecotes, which come in all shapes and sizes, sometimes adjacent to country manors, are worthy of note. Enticing pigeons to roost, they played a vital role in the supply of essential protein in a restricted diet.

Ancient bridges reveal wonderful examples of medieval stonework, and sometimes depicted thereon are emblems (such as lovers' knots) of the local aristocracy – as found at Blatherwycke. Many of these bridges had curious 'legacies', like Kislingbury bridge, for which 'a heyffor of 5 years with a white baby' was bequeathed for the purpose of maintenance. Note, too, the very practical cutwaters, built to protect the stone footings by cutting the heavy flow of water in times of flood. This is evident in the long arched bridge span at Wansford in the north of the county.

Unique wrought-iron gates and pillars, often topped by griffins or flamboyant birds, either perched or in flight, as the white swans at Lamport Hall, also have a fascinating tale to tell.

Treasures aplenty abound in our shire, but as you wander up hill and down dale, watch out for the lurking potholes and take heed where you put that stout stick.

Above all else – CHERISH THE COUNTRYSIDE!

Mia Butler
June 1996

Cosgrove

Cosgrove is 12 miles from Northampton, and about three-quarters of a mile east of the A508 just before it reaches Watling Street (A5). The village was bisected by the construction of the Grand Union Canal in the 1800s and consequently there is no through road. It has now become a popular leisure area and there is a caravan park based around several lakes – the aftermath of sand and gravel extraction. Gaily painted narrow-boats are frequently moored along the canal banks in summer.

Compact is the word to describe this charming little circuit situated well down in the southerly sector of the county, close to the border with Buckinghamshire. Because of its peripheral position, the spot is perhaps lesser known to those living in the county's middle and northern parts.

The entire circuit is about half a mile, with no stiles, but one flight of steps. It can quite easily be split into two walks, as it is a figure of eight whose handy pivot is the pub.

The Gothic style bridge which spans the Grand Union Canal.

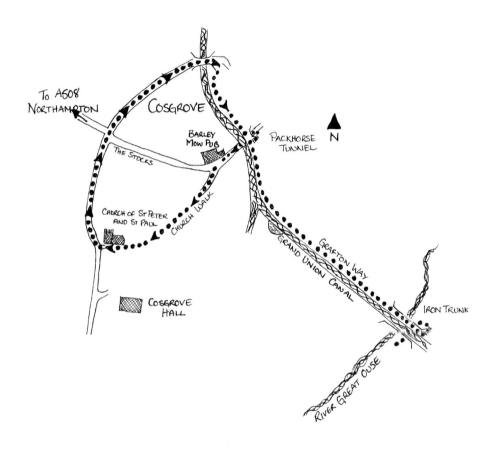

The walk begins at The Barley Mow public house. Cross the lane (to the west), making for the iron kissing-gate and fenced Church Walk bordering the field, under the bulging stone wall, towards the church of St Peter and St Paul. The fourteenth century tower houses six bells and has an elegant round copper-faced clock. Note the cobblestones outside the porch and the old-fashioned metal foot-scraper (and use it if necessary!). If you are lucky enough to gain access, the scarlet lined door and carpet make a wonderful contrast to the sombre interior.

Leave the churchyard by the black iron gates and glance at the eighteenth century Cosgrove Hall and outbuildings. Follow the wall around Medlar House, the former rectory, downhill to The Stocks.

Straight on now to the fine bridge spanning the canal, repaired not long ago with reconstituted stone. At the far end of the parapet, go down the slope to the towpath and continue as far as the steps on the left bank. Now for a surprise. Go sharp left at the foot of these steps and through the 'cattle-creep' or packhorse tunnel, under the water! As daylight appears again, trudge up the gentle slope to see The Barley Mow on the corner.

If you feel adventurous and would like to see another unique spot (OK for wheelchairs), carry on past the canal-side steps on the

The Iron Trunk aqueduct at Cosgrove carrying the Grand Union Canal over the Great Ouse.

towpath, passing the wide 'turning pool' and the defunct Old
Stratford and Buckingham Arm of the canal. Keep going, now on
the Grafton Way to the famous Iron Trunk, where the water is
carried directly over the River Great Ouse far below. This feat of
engineering was originally constructed of wood, but after its
collapse in 1808 the present cast-iron version replaced it. The truly
unique aqueduct, 101 feet long and 15 feet wide, is supported on
stout pillars and may be viewed from the river bank via a second
tunnel.

Nearby: Motte and bailey medieval site at Old Wolverton, Bucks.

Braunston

Braunston, another canal site, is on the A45, 15 miles from Coventry and four miles from Daventry. Many of the narrow-boats moored along the waterside are colourfully painted in traditional canal art style, with the on-board pots and utensils similarly decorated. Windows proudly show fringed or tasselled trimmings, and sometimes dainty crocheted coverings enhance the brass ringed portholes. The stout rope fenders on the boats were very often locally made, though this is, sadly, a declining trade.

A word of warning! Access to footbridges and towpaths is frequently steep and not necessarily paved. Footpaths to and from the village are firm, but with considerable slopes. There are no stiles, but the going is not suited to wheelchairs. Beware of mooring ropes and rings on the towpaths.

The circuit is roughly one mile.

The Horseley iron footbridge at Braunston.

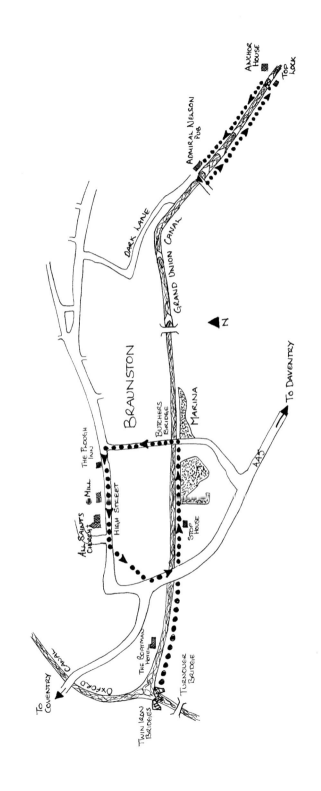

The walk starts at the marina where the white-painted Horseley iron footbridge spans what used to be the entrance to the Northern Oxford Canal from the Grand Union Canal (London to Birmingham). Developments now skirting the busy marina include housing – as well as the boatyards, etc., catering for the various needs of the waterways users. Additional facilities, such as cruises, are available to visitors in summer. On the towpath, go to the right beside 'short stay moorings' on the shady path. Signs at Butchers Bridge indicate services further on, but ignore these and go up and over to the uphill footpath. Do turn to admire the view over the rural landscape and basin, fashioned from the former reservoirs adjacent to the canal.

At Nibbits Lane, join the High Street and bear left opposite 'The Village Bakery' sign on the facing wall, and pass the pretty facade of The Plough Inn. There is a pleasant mix of both brick and stone dwellings, including the lovely Mill House where the unique brick tower-mill rises from the background, not far from the impressive church.

All Saints occupies a prominent position and has done so since Norman times. Rebuilt for the third time in 1849, it exudes a tranquil ambience, with its combined pale hues of grey Weldon and brown Duston sandstone. It is light and airy inside, with many stained glass and clear windows, and stone flags and tiles on the floor. The pink Derbyshire marble and white alabaster pulpit and the font of Derbyshire, Devon and Sicillian marble (1800) catch the eye. Relics from an earlier church include a stunning stone effigy of a man in ringtail armour. He is portrayed lying curiously cross-legged, with scabbard and shield, and is thought to be William de Ros, a Knight who perished en route for the Holy Land in 1352. An ancient parish chest with three heavy locks for protection, stored important documents and ensured safe keeping.

A seat in the grassy churchyard, set above the war memorial, affords a splendid panorama over the neighbouring Warwickshire countryside. Almost opposite, a fingerpost points the way downhill on a hard path, to exit on the verge of the busy A45, at a bus stop and seat opposite The Mill House (formerly The Boatman Hotel). Cross the road with care to descend to the bank.

A medieval stone effigy in All Saints church, Braunston.

For a fascinating extension to your ramble (or separate linear excursion excluding the village loop):

Turn left on the towpath towards the hotel and only just around the bend, out of sight, is a setting well worth the effort. Twin iron Horseley bridges, identified as by the Black Country manufacturers, link to form three arches and mark the junction of the Oxford Canal. From here, see the fine example of the 'turn-over bridge' beside the site of ancient fish-ponds, where horses towing the early barges could negotiate the ramps to change sides without being unhitched.

If you choose not to make the detour, turn under the A45 canal side towards The Stop House, constructed in 1796 and where tolls were collected up to the last century. The building was reopened in 1990 as an office and exhibition centre for British Waterways (open 9.00 am to 4.30 pm weekdays, and afternoons only on summer Sundays and Bank Holidays). Information can be found here about the free use of mooring bollards for disabled boaters.

A further option:

On the village side of the canal, follow the High Street to the last downhill turning, Dark Lane, and carry on to its conclusion at The Admiral Nelson public house which, incidentally, is said to be haunted!

Turn over the bridge and walk the towpath by three locks and up the ramp, leaving the water at the fourth. The British Waterways sign records the six lock flight and its fall of 10.8 metres. Cross the bridge to Anchor House and return via the bridleway to the pub, with sight of the village ahead on the skyline. Take care over three traffic humps.

Nearby: Daventry Country Park.

Cogenhoe

The village of Cogenhoe is about six miles east of the county town and signposted from the A45. Known as 'Kukenhoe' in the mid-thirteenth century, it is now more often pronounced 'Cookno'.

Standing proud on the hill is the church of St Peter, built by Nicholas of Cogenhoe and completed about 1290. The effigy of the knight within is thought to be that of the benefactor.

From the main street, Station Road, turn into Church Street opposite The Royal Oak public house. As the lane narrows, a small triangular green comes into sight, where it changes to Mill Lane on the lower side. The walk begins here, so please be aware of the local residents' needs and park with discretion.

The circuit is approximately a quarter mile. There are no stiles but fairly steep slopes exist in both directions.

Follow the Nene Way posts and discs downhill under a high stone wall and along a quaint hidden alleyway to a gate giving access to a downward sloping undulating meadow.

As you proceed, look back at the church on the rise, and then forward over the sweep of the Nene Valley. Ecton can now be seen on the far side of the valley, and also the ancient Saxon tower of All Saints church at Earls Barton. All the time the constant hum of traffic on the A45 hangs in the air. Make for the exit gate to the lane by the tall trees.

For a slightly extended version of the walk, visiting an ancient packbridge, take the path that leads straight ahead. Follow the public right of way through Cogenhoe Mill Caravan Park, where first the Nene Way departs alongside a garage to hug the riverbank and leads towards Whiston Mill. Carry on over the millstream and past Mill House to the lock.

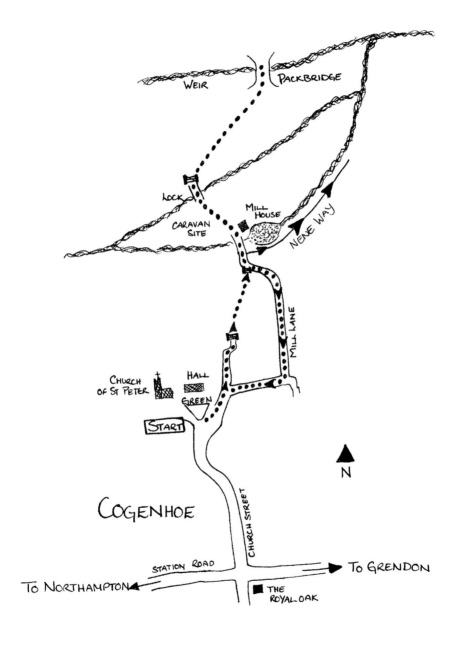

Take heed of the English Heritage/Countryside Commission notice about access to the riverside which is fixed by the iron gate, almost opposite the weir. Walk across the field, heading a little to the right. The twin-arched stone packbridge spans Back Brook. It was probably constructed over the original watercourse before later diversions made way for barges in the heyday of the waterways. A closer look will show where the cobbles underfoot have been worn smooth by man and beast over the centuries. (This footpath continues to Ecton.)

The twin-arched stone packbridge over Back Brook at Cogenhoe

Return now, back across the recreational site, round by Crossing Cottage on the curve and walk up the lane, watching out for any vehicles. Note the sign at the Anglian Water depot 'Private road – no vehicular access except for patrons of Cogenhoe Mill'. The Green is further up the hill and around the corner, where a short path, topside, leads directly to the church.

Nearby: Castle Ashby Gardens, Tea Room and Shopping Yard.

Pitsford Water

Pitsford village is accessible from the A508 Northampton to Market Harborough road or from Kettering by the A43 via Holcot and Brixworth by-pass.

If you like wide open spaces and uncluttered rolling vistas, then this is for you. Bear in mind that this waterside walk can be chilly and breezy in less than perfect weather, but on a warm sunny day, it can be quite invigorating!

Whatever the time of year, the contours and shades of the surrounding slopes are a constant treat, as the copses, hedgerows and fields resemble a patchwork quilt.

Well-known as an area for leisure and recreation, this fantastic stretch of water offers facilities for anglers, sailboat enthusiasts, bird-watchers, lovers of wildlife, walkers and a splendid location for a picnic.

Construction of the reservoir began in 1952 and it was officially opened by HM The Queen Mother in 1956. It was built and is maintained to supply mains water, and the entire zone is now designated an SSSI (Site of Special Scientific Interest). The basic circular walk is short, but it may easily be extended with little extra effort to provide greater interest and perhaps an element of excitement. The extension takes you over the wide 'steps' of the overflow – dry when water levels are low, but in winter the torrent gushes down under your feet.

The long dam ($3/4$ mile return) is totally flat, between protective walls, and might be an unusual adventure for some. The draw-off tower is also worth a look if you have never had the opportunity of a 'close encounter' with this water supply vital to all.

In the village of Pitsford, follow the signpost at the triangle

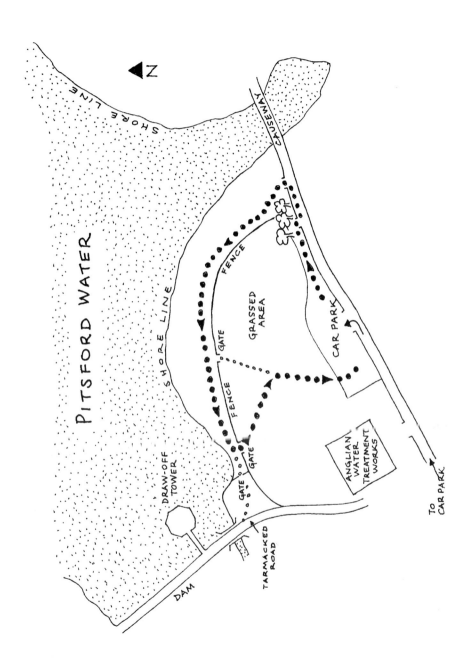

'Reservoir Car Park – No Through Road' and beware of speed-bumps in the narrow lane as you pass through a leafy tunnel of trees. Carry on past the gates of Anglian Water, up the hill to the car park and picnic site overlooking the reservoir and the vast expanse of glorious countryside slanting down to the water's edge. Leaving your car, walk down through the gap in the hedge on the lower (right) side down the path through the car park and briefly out into the lane. The little causeway is a handy place from which to admire the scenery and take one's bearings. The small lake may be teeming with wildlife (though not necessarily visible!) in that enchanting secluded sanctuary.

Picnic beside Pitsford Water.

Look around and back up the lane at the mass of mature trees, which include field maple and sycamore. Pass through the iron handgate on the near side of the causeway, under the willows and traverse the grassy slightly elevated path on the outer edge of the fence, to enjoy unrestricted views. A plethora of water-birds – such as coot, mallard and grebe – abound in summer and, of course, species vary with the changing seasons.

Follow the curve of the bank as far as it goes. A couple of gates then lead to paths up the steep pull back to the car park.

To extend the walk, approach the double gates and observe the notices posted on the perimeter fence. On the far side, sailboats are much in evidence, and behind the stand of trees is Brixworth Country Park with its many facilities.

Go forward on to the dam proper, on a good flat surface, crossing the overflow, and on past the draw-off tower. To leave the dam at the other end, a stile has to be considered and negotiated. Return from this point.

Viewed from the higher level, Brixworth sprawls across the horizon, and the spire of All Saints church, said to be the most imposing architectural memorial 'north of the Alps', pierces the skyline.

The overflow and the draw-off tower at Pitsford Reservoir.

Nearby: Northampton and Lamport Railway at Brampton Halt, reached by crossing directly over the A508 toward Chapel Brampton. Enquiries 01604 320327.

Ecton

Turn off the A4500 from Wellingborough 3½ miles east of Northampton at the World's End, where it is said that the original pub sign was painted by the eminent artist Hogarth and taken by the landlord in repayment of a debt!

This is essentially a concise circuit in a compact village with historical connections and of considerable charm. OK for wheelchairs and under half a mile.

A leisurely stroll will surely reap rewards, as the evocative nooks and crannies reveal secluded gardens and miniature courtyards. The mellowed limestone and thatched roofs of the older dwellings lend pleasing tones and immense character to the scene. Do allow time to savour the delights and nuances en route.

Start at the 'dead end' of West Street, at the field gate from where there is an enticing view of the sweep of the Nene Valley over to Cogenhoe. Please park tidily.

Facing the gate and red phone box in the private garden to the left, turn into the short alleyway alongside moss-topped walls. To one side is a grand old stone barn, and to the other a pair of pretty brick cottages. Here, too, note the solid square tower of the thirteenth-century church, with a weather vane on each corner.

Taking the uphill path, cameos of partly hidden corners and patios tempt the observer and, in summer, will especially fascinate the gardener.

Opposite Wheelwrights Cottage, the Three Horseshoes pub, with a painted sign, was built on the site of the former smithy, owned by the ancestors of Benjamin Franklyn, whose family also operated the bell foundry. Josiah Franklyn, his father, had

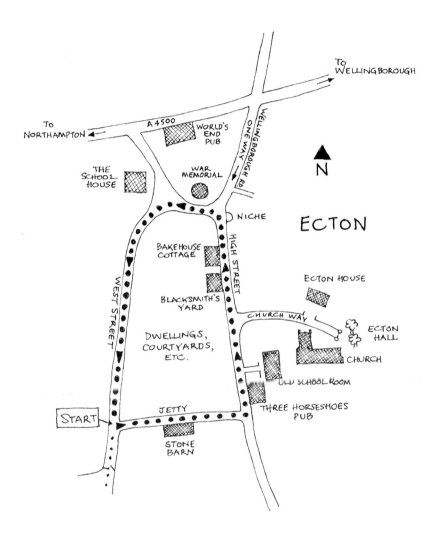

emigrated to Boston in 1862, previously living here in Savins Yard with his family.

American Benjamin Franklyn, scholar, scientist, author, inventor and statesman, was a Founding Father, involved with the framing of the Constitution of America.

Just beyond the pub, set back on the front wall of a house is the inscription 'School for poor children', which was founded in 1752 by John Palmer, linguist and rector of this parish, and from a local prominent family.

Church Way opens to the seventeenth-century Ecton House, the old rectory, also built by John Palmer, now an ecclesiastical retreat and conference centre.

Ecton Hall, constructed of light sandstone, now converted to a private residence, is hidden behind greenery beyond the pillars of an imposing gateway.

Tranquillity in Ecton High Street.

A bronze plaque and bust of Benjamin Franklyn in the church of St Mary Magdalene was presented by a group of Americans in 1910. The famous man's relatives rest in the graveyard.

Seek out the curious scratch dial on the south porch, a relic of the past, although now somewhat eroded by the elements. A gnomon (or stick) was fixed to the central hole to indicate the hour (on scratched lines) for worship.

The scratch dial on the south porch of St Mary Magdelene in Ecton.

The secret corners, Blacksmiths Yard, Bakehouse Cottage and an iron lamppost, enhance the picturesque High Street, and near the road sign is a niche low in the stone wall, perhaps a reminder of the numerous wells used by the early inhabitants.

At the start of the one-way Wellingborough Road, up stone steps, the War Memorial bears the poignant message 'Ecton not unmindful'.

Carry on left into West Street in front of The School House, with its doorways marked 'Girls and Infants' and 'Boys Entrance' to the later houses, where an air of serenity still persists, past the Old Bakehouse and the Old Chapel.

Return to start.

The whole ambience is, refreshingly, one of obvious pride in the community, where rubbish and graffiti are pleasantly absent.

Note: You may be tempted to go forward through the kissing-gate, following the line of the fingerpost. However, in crossing the first field, a stile ahead is on the boundary of the Cricket Field; the path merges into the lane just outside the village. This does provide a pleasant extension to the walk but is unsuitable for the infirm.

Nearby: Sywell Country Park. Enquiries 01604 810970.

Geddington

Geddington, laced with history, is four miles north of Kettering on the A43 – turning at Queen Street or West Street – where a royal hunting lodge once stood in the midst of the dense and vast Rockingham Forest. Hunting was reserved for the 'Monarch's pleasure', and the slaughter of a deer by a peasant was punishable by death!

Designated a Conservation Area in 1977, Geddington's centrepiece is its Eleanor Cross erected at the order of Edward I around 1294 in memory of his queen, Eleanor of Castile, who had died in 1290 at Harby in Nottinghamshire. The funeral cortege, en route for London, made overnight stops at many places, including Geddington, where later such crosses were to be erected. This monument is now the most splendid of the remaining three and stands at the heart of the community.

In close proximity is the church of St Mary Magdalene, which has traces of a Saxon nave, where the queen's body would have lain. The handsome thirteenth-century bridge nearby, with its three protective cutwaters, must have been crossed by the funeral procession as it set out on the next stage of the slow progression to the capital and the Queen's final resting place.

This is, indeed, a fascinating setting, and if you wish to saunter no further, but simply admire the view, then on summer weekends a very civilised teashop is conveniently placed opposite the cross. A massive and mysterious boulder hunches here against the wall.

The circuit is less than a mile on flat ground and suitable for wheelchairs.

Start the walk at the Eleanor Cross, the focal point, with The Star opposite. Two information boards, one at the foot of the steps and

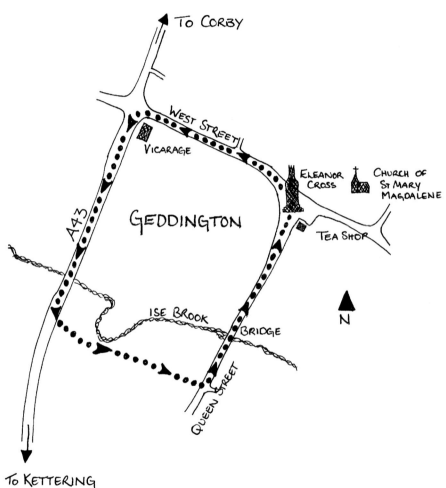

The Eleanor Cross at Geddington.

the other over the road at the corner of Church Hill and Grafton Road, near Blacksmith's Cottage, provide a comprehensive guide to the immediate surroundings.

Turn uphill into West Street, where The Maltings, Wormleighton Way and Lee's Way tempt the walker with intriguing alleyways and glimpses of thatched cottages and secluded yards. Another pub is along here, too –The White Hart – and soon after, the rambling old vicarage built in 1851, with its angular chimneys and sturdy outbuildings. William Gladstone, a past Liberal Prime Minister, and other prominent citizens, received their early education here when it was a preparatory school.

At the crossroads, turn left on to New Road (A43 Kettering to Corby), passing the bus stop and on to the balustraded bridge over the River Ise.

At the finger post, turn down the bank to the meadows. Here there are seats, handsome gnarled willows, iron lampposts and a memorial plaque to Walter John, Duke of Buccleuch 'who loved the countryside'. The path continues past an attractive row of restored cottages to emerge beside the United Reformed chapel, and the Post Office and Village Hall complex over the road.

The ford and thirteenth-century bridge, with the ducks, in Queen Street, Geddington.

Turn left now towards the lovely old bridge mentioned earlier, where assorted ducks are often paddling in and out of the shallow ford – a pleasant place to lean and linger en route for the Cross just ahead. (Light vehicles only may now use this ancient bridge).

Nearby: Boughton House (The Living Landscape Trust)
Phone: 01536 515731

Cranford

Cranford is between Kettering (three miles away) and Thrapston (five miles away) off the A14. Mentioned in the Domesday Book, Cranford is made up of two parishes, St John and St Andrew, linked by glorious typically English parkland – the main feature of this particular walk. Fortunately, with the construction of the nearby A14, heavy traffic no longer trundles through the village, which has regained its once tranquil ambience.

It is flat surfaces all the way on this walk, with no stiles.

Start at the Village Hall in Grafton Road, which bears a memorial tablet (dated 1896) to Sir Frederick Laud Robinson, ninth Baronet, and stands at the corner of traditional sweeping parkland.

Walk down the path, with open views on either side and passing white gates, to the stone bridge overhung by willows. On the raised pathway, ignore the fingerpost at too awkward a stile. Look over to the lovely tableau of the church and the elegant eighteenth century Cranford Hall, veiled by mature trees. The seat on the hill might prove handy for a breather.

At the T-junction with the High Street, do take a moment to admire the stone houses and cottages, particularly the dwelling with the striking porch and gable end window. Remains of an old pump are left beside a cottage wall, and the Baptist chapel is on the opposite side of the road.

Carry on as far as the phone box, bus stop and seat, under the spreading chestnut tree, with The Red Lion pub nearby. Turn left here, following the low wall, perhaps to linger at The Green to savour the peace and quiet, now in the parish of St John. On this row is the store and Post Office, which has a quaint gable end wall where the original holes of the pigeon loft are still in evidence.

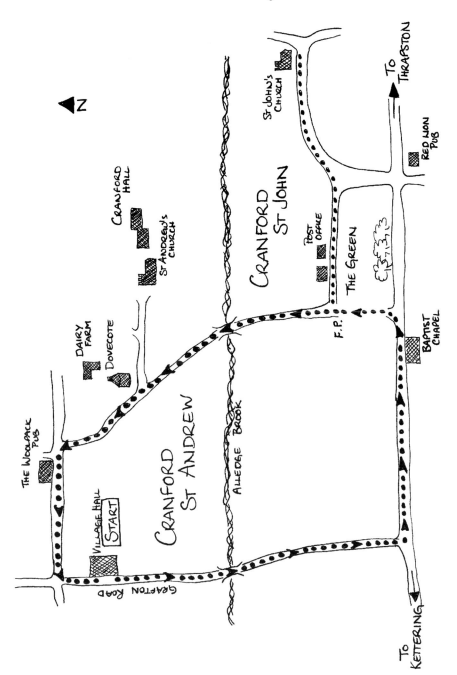

Inclination and a little energy will be rewarded in further exploration of this area, by going into Church Lane to the medieval church of St John on the corner of Duck End. Homes of all shapes and sizes line the lane, one of banded stone and many with moss blotched roof tiles which lend mellow hues.

Otherwise, continue the walk at The Green by the double fingerpost, staying on the path beside the slatted fence. Watch out for the odd pheasant disturbed by human presence!

The decorative iron bridge over Alledge Brook commemorates 'HM Diamond Jubilee 1897' and opens to sheep grazing pastoral beauty, studded with majestic trees, in this perfect rural setting.

A cameo of rural England at Cranford.

Follow the path which branches off to St Andrews church, of twelfth century origin, but now sadly redundant. The stunning circular dovecote, thought to be from the fifteenth century (Heritage Site), stands in the grounds of Dairy Farm, a seventeenth century thatched Jacobean manor house.

Exit from the parkland through the white handgate ahead to emerge almost opposite The Woolpack pub in St Andrew's Lane,

The circular dovecote in the grounds of Dairy Farm at Cranford.

and return to the start point where the dilapidated old blacksmith's shop stands near the Village Hall, just out of sight around the corner.

Kinewell Lake

The tranquil setting of Kinewell Lake, in care of the Kinewell Lake Trust, is the venue for the longest walk in this series, of just under 1½ miles and situated to the west of Ringstead.

One of our county's numerous Pocket Parks (mentioned at the end of the book), this haven for wildlife may be enjoyed as a complete circular walk, following the obvious trail, or there is the opportunity for a short stroll along the banks, conveniently dotted with picnic sets and well placed seats.

Whatever your countryside pleasure may be, this 80-acre site allows access to a remarkable variety of natural habitats, where fishing is only available to local villagers and club members.

An information board in the main car park provides a useful guide to wildlife in its many forms at this splendid lake dotted with islands, which was formed naturally in 1979 following a lengthy period of gravel extraction. Beware of tacky conditions which may be encountered in the wet winter months. Binoculars would be an advantage and there is easy access to the hide, constructed and donated by a local company. Be on the lookout for goldfinch, goldeneye, pochard, heron, tufted duck, great crested grebe and many more colourful birds, both resident and migratory. An abundance of flora enhances the lakeside slopes where flimsy dragonflies and damselflies hover and myriad butterflies flit over summer flowers seeking sustaining nectar.

On leaving the car park on the outskirts of Ringstead village, walk on the broad track in an anti-clockwise direction. A footpath and stile lead back toward the line of houses, and the short, broach spire of the church of St Mary peeps over the rooftops.

A slight bump next, as the reed-fringed shore curves and butts a

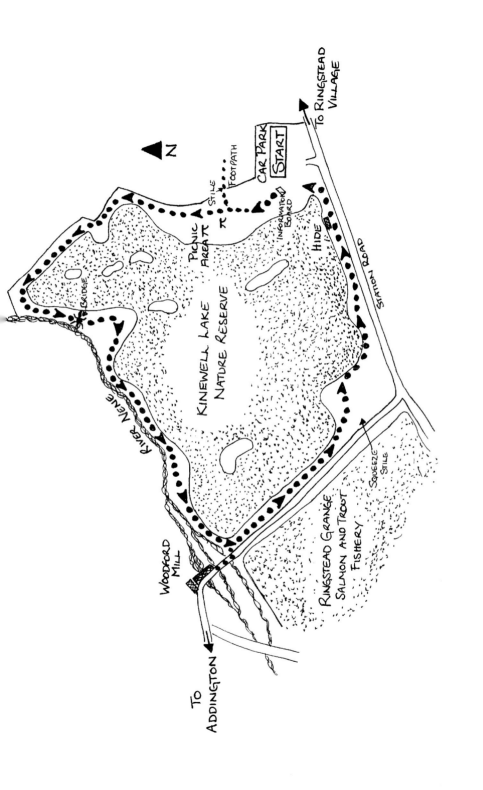

ditch before continuing, edged by bushes and much willow over the water. The occasional waymark disc shows the way, although the path is recognisable and hardly deviates. As it turns towards the river and then runs parallel to it, the wooden footbridge spans a narrow culvert, then running beneath a tall stand of trees. On the opposite bank, particularly at the weekend when a match may be in progress, patient fishermen sit and ponder.

Very soon Woodford Mill comes into sight, known locally as Willy Watt Mill mentioned in the Domesday Book, where boats of all shapes and sizes are moored or await their turn through the lock.

The view from the bridge at Woodford Mill.

One may exit here to the road and two bridges, to look over the parapet at the rushing water below and return via the road. The raised footway of wooden planks is not to be recommended for those not sure of foot. This is another relic of the past, constructed when the waters of the valley were not controlled as today, when this section was frequently flooded.

Pause for reflection?

Just prior to the T-junction, a 'squeeze-stile' allows re-entry to the lakeside, but first, look out over the vast expanse of the fishery (see below), where the honks, hoots, hisses and squawks of the waterbirds rend the otherwise peaceful air.

Stay on the grass track past the boomerang-shaped plantation and more belts of weeping willow on the hem of the water, as it winds around back to the hide and car park.

Nearby: Ringstead Grange and Salmon Trout Fishery.

East Carlton

The park is situated just off the north side of the A427 Corby to Market Harborough road and west of Corby. East Carlton Countryside Park covers an area of 100 acres of parkland dotted with lofty trees, and features an impressive Hall in red brick and ironstone, resembling the style of a French chateau, built on the site of an earlier mansion and now a private residence. The setting is altogether beautiful, with the sweeping vista over the Welland Valley providing a delight as the hills appear in folds against the horizon.

There is a craft workshop, converted from the eighteenth century coach-house, where artisans may be seen at work. Adjacent is the Steel Heritage Centre, which graphically illustrates the history of the steel industry for which nearby Corby is famed. Massive pieces of equipment are on display outside, including a giant dragline bucket used in the quarries in the 1950s, and huge ingots of steel, the product of that era.

Facilities include a cafeteria with seating inside, and outside on the spacious forecourt where one may enjoy the scenery. Another feature for children of all ages is a static full-size brightly-painted steam locomotive for clambering and climbing on, and there is a jolly playground, picnic area and wishing-well. Plenty of space exists for games, with adequate seating, car parking and toilets (including for the disabled).

It is the venue for many outdoor summer activities and events, usually advertised locally, and maps and leaflets are available covering the different aspects of the area.

Begin the circular walk at the Heritage Centre. You may prefer to simply follow the hard paths laid around the park to see the ponds and handsome tree specimens, some exotic; or perhaps pursue the Nature Trail.

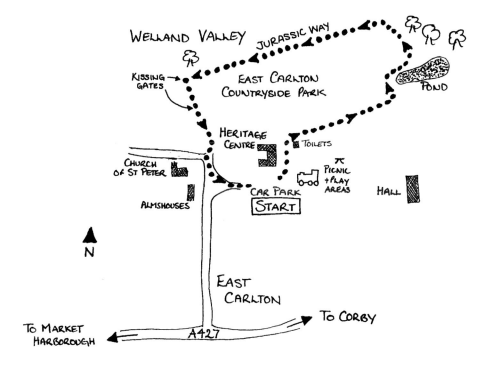

The gentle slopes of the Welland Valley.

However, to enjoy the valley with an unrestricted view, take the path alongside the play patch down towards the pond, but branching off to the left just before it, skirting the water. Look out for the miscellany of waterbirds, which may vary from season to season, although residents such as mallards, coots and moorhens will invariably be actively engaged in one way or another. Exit by the boundary gate beside the brook overshadowed by beech trees, from where you can see distant villages nestling against the rolling hills of Leicestershire.

Turn sharp left briefly to join the Jurassic Way (another long-distance county footpath) as far as the lone oak tree. A kissing-gate here leads into a sloping meadow in a corner of the park.

Carry on up the incline, keeping parallel with the hedge and through a further kissing-gate. A disc on the iron railing on the driveway directs the walker to the exit at a bend in the lane.

The solid church of St Peter, an eighteenth century replica of the original, stands high on the hill, with a horse-trough in the outer wall. Adjacent are the genteel almshouses, rebuilt in 1866 in the Tudor style, bearing a plaque 'Hospital of the Blessed Jesus in

Carlton' founded by Sir Geoffrey Palmer, Bart., inscribed with the seventeenth-century date and details of endowment.

Return to the park through decorative spiked iron gates by Gimson and Co. of Leicester to a short avenue of cherry and crab-apple trees.

No charge to ride on this loco!

Addendum: Since this book was first researched the boundary gate mentioned on page 44 has been sealed, leaving only a stile for exit at this point.

Nearby: Rockingham Castle. Enquiries 01536 770240.

Aldwincle

The location of this walk is two miles north of Thrapston on the A605, turning off at Thorpe Waterville. Lowick Lane is first left on entering Aldwincle. Follow this to the car park at the Titchmarsh Nature Reserve on the left.

The car park affords extensive views over the reserve and heronry and has a comprehensive information board for the benefit of visitors. Owned and managed by The Wildlife Trust, spreading over 180 acres and in part an SSSI (Site of Special Scientific Interest), the area is now well established as a mecca for birdwatchers, nature lovers and walkers, as the Nene Way links through to Thrapston. The lakes are the aftermath of gravel

Baulks Lane at Aldwincle.

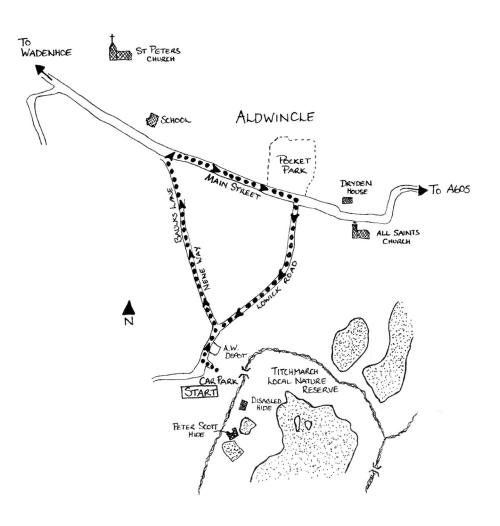

workings, similar to others in the valley. Migrant waders, such as redshank and greenshank, briefly feed on the muddy banks, and flocks of ducks and coots overwinter here. Several hides exist, and one of these is sponsored by Oundle School in memory of Sir Peter Scott, who frequented this spot when a pupil there. Another hide is specifically designed to enhance observation by wheelchair visitors.

A waderscrape and islands have been gradually added over the years, to extend this wildlife refuge. The Heronry was planted by Lord Lilford in 1885 as a duck decoy, where now nesting herons may breed in isolation, undisturbed. (No access to site allowed).

Those with a passion for insects will appreciate the diverse species of butterflies breeding on the covering flora, as well as the astonishing plethora of other winged insects.

During gravel extraction a Roman bridge and causeway was discovered, which will have carried the Roman Gartree road to Leicester over the River Nene.

This is a short walk of about half a mile, and can be negotiated by wheelchairs.

On leaving the car park turn right into Lowick lane, past the Anglian Water enclosure, to the bottom of Baulks Lane, flanked by attractive houses and gardens. Walk up through the cutting, now on a section of the long-distance Nene Way, beside a stand of stately poplars and grassy banks, to the top where a seat bears notice of the 1977 Jubilee. Turn right on to Main Street as far as the Pocket Park, a quiet and secluded dell. Just ahead is Dryden House (the Old Rectory) to remind us that John Dryden, Poet Laureate to the Crown, was born here in 1631 and christened just along the road at All Saints church, now redundant since 1879.

Another literary figure of repute, Thomas Fuller, was born in the village in 1608 in a former rectory, long since demolished. He was to become a historian, Doctor of Divinity, and author of *The Worthies of England* and was appointed Chaplain to King Charles II.

Turn into Lowick Lane, which has been severely narrowed, so beware of passing traffic. A plaque dated 1834 on the wall of

Vista from the Nature Reserve with the redundant church of All Saints on the skyline.

Tavern Cottage bears a Latin inscription which, translated, reads 'Believers in Christ have eternal life'. Carry on to return to the car park.

Nearby: Old market town of Thrapston.

Wadenhoe

This walk – to the west of the A605 Thrapston to Oundle road, turning off at Thorpe Waterville, via Aldwincle – is partly through the village, and partly circles around on fieldpaths where the going is steep.

Wadenhoe is a gem among villages, where even the more recent history is faithfully recorded for posterity. In the church of St Michael and All Angels, with the distinctive saddleback roof over the late Norman tower, is a poignant memorial to a young couple on honeymoon in Italy. Thomas Hunt, owner of the manor, and his bride Caroline Isham, daughter of the rector of Polebrook, were tragically murdered in 1824.

A later member of the same family, the Rt Hon. George Ward-Hunt, was Chancellor of the Exchequer in Disraeli's Cabinet in 1868 and had the earliest rural postal telegraph office installed in order to keep in contact with the affairs of the government. He became First Lord of the Admiralty in 1874 and was the innovator of the local gasworks which lit the streets and dwellings. The site was where the present Village Hall stands.

The walk is about half a mile, with gates, and not suitable for wheelchairs away from the streets.

Begin at the Village Hall beside the river where, in summer, teas are usually served to visitors on Sundays. Boats come and go through the lock, and a seat on the bank offers a grandstand view. A handy place, too, to observe the lacy-winged dragonflies in their season.

The charming cottages here and The Kings Head public house, with gardens flowing down to the water's edge, are on the rise, so look out for the birds nests tucked away beneath the eaves. At the

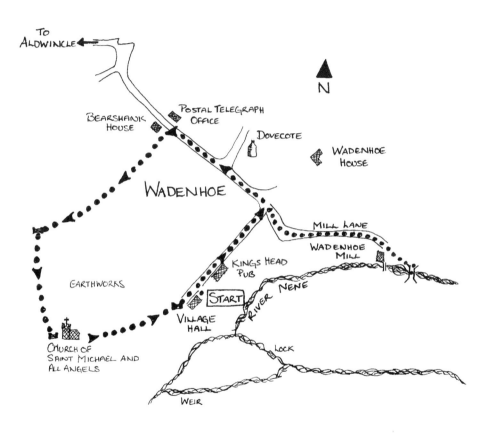

top of the lane, facing, is a unique building, similar in design to a tollhouse.

To avoid the field walking, a stroll down Mill Lane, to the right, following the high boundary wall of Wadenhoe House, will reveal the delightful setting of Wadenhoe Mill, which occupies the spot where once stood an early mill, mentioned in the Domesday Book. This route is also on the Nene Way, over the wooden footbridge of the shallow ford, across the water meadows to Thorpe Achurch in the distance.

To resume the circuit, turn left at the pretty house and just around the bend on the right, note the circular limestone dovecote with a roof of Collyweston slate standing in the stable-yard. It is thought to date from the eighteenth century and is now a County Heritage site.

The 'Postal Telegraph Office' at Wadenhoe

Turn back to the 'up' street to the 'Postal Telegraph Office', mentioned previously, opposite the handsome, stone Bearshank House, with a recessed gate and waymark beside the garage. Turn through here into the fields, passing a sunken stone outcrop and

Wadenhoe Mill.

going downhill in the next pasture on the Lyvden Way, crossing midfield at the bottom to avoid the ditch.

On the hill the church stands alone, but the adjoining earthworks are purported to be the site of a bygone community and indicates a windmill mound. There are beautiful views here on the downward path and seats to enjoy a rest and admire the broad stretch of the Nene Valley and intriguing glimpses of the river winding below. The sound of rushing water from the weir grows near as the steep path ends at the weighted gate to the Village Hall.

Barnwell

Barnwell is on the eastern side of the A605, south of Oundle. This neat and easy circuit of approximately a quarter mile, with no stiles, has great rewards even in winter, when the bare branches of the trees enable the walker to look across to the imposing ramparts of Barnwell Castle. Built in the thirteenth century for Berengarious le Moine and viewed from several angles en route, the mass of trees enhance the mighty ruins which still exude an air of mystery. Indeed, they are said to be haunted by a monk brandishing a whip!

Barnwell Manor, adjacent to the castle, was formerly the royal residence of the Duke and Duchess of Gloucester, whose gardens are usually open to the public on two or three days each year (see the National Gardens leaflet).

Turn off the A605 at the Old Station House, long since deprived of its railway line, and turn right at the village sign, going towards St Andrews church, where the walk begins.

Almost opposite are the old almshouses, bearing an informative stone tablet recording the endowment of Latham's Almshouses, founded in 1601 and rebuilt in 1874. The Reverend Nicholas Latham was also responsible for the first school in the community and is remembered by a monument (1620) in the church. Carry on down the hill towards the stone bridge and sight of The Montagu Arms hostelry. Just before the crossing veer slightly to the left, skirting a cluster of five tall lime trees to tread the wooden bridge over the brook. (For a longer loop to All Saints chapel, guardian of the Montagu family vault and memorials, turn to the right alongside the stream.)

Keep to the left, passing 'The Reading Room' and along the

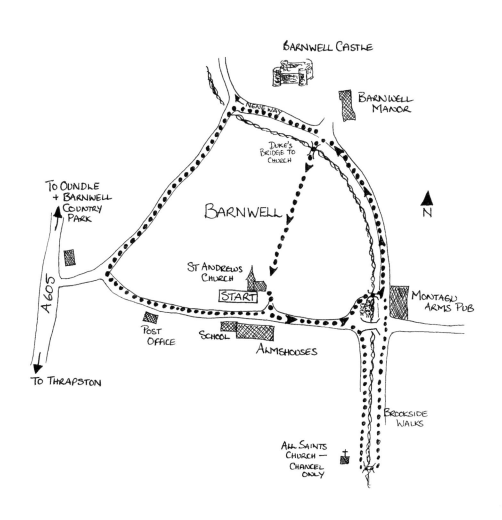

bank of the stream lined with willows. High on the brow of the hill, the commanding ruins of Barnwell Castle dominate the scene, the thick walls and towers dwarfing all else, standing over the dignified Elizabethan Manor House. A further extension may be taken by keeping straight on along the Nene Way as far as the T-junction (giving a better view of the castle), and left again up the hill to complete the circuit.

Looking back through a willow veil at Barnwell Manor.

In this idyllic setting, pause and cross the charming little footbridge constructed to provide a handy path, for a former duke, from the manor to the church, bordered by beech trees. The iron handgate and steps lead the way into the churchyard and a look at the narrow priests' door. On the north doorway is a medieval reminder of a May Day custom – the green man, his face sprouting with leaves, a symbol of spring and regeneration, when the boys ogled the girls, camouflaging themselves with leaves! High on the south side, the corbel-frieze has an intriguing row of heads, both human and animal, and a less ancient sundial. There is a splendid round window encircled by a dog-tooth design, and low

St Andrew's Church, Barnwell.

down beside the porch is a benchmark.

Note the novel sliding knob on the heavy door, opening to reveal a wealth of fascinating features inside. The adjoining wall has, in part, scant remains from All Saints church, both buildings dating from the thirteenth century.

Nearby: Barnwell Country Park and the ancient town of Oundle.

Country Parks

BARNWELL
A small, compact park with differing habitats, developed after extensive gravel extraction, resulting in four lakes and islands, covering 37 acres (15 hectares). Opened in 1971, it has a Visitor Centre and toilet facilities for the disabled. Day permit required for fishing. Situated south of Oundle on the old A605 to Thrapston.
Tel: 01832 273435.

BRAMPTON VALLEY WAY
A linear park stretching over 14 miles (22km) based on the former Northampton to Market Harborough railway line linking the two towns. First section opened in 1989. Excellent for spotting wildlife of all kinds. Starting from Boughton Crossing, off the A50 north of the county town, there are a number of access points to the trail which is stoned in part, with car parks and picnic sites en route.
Tel: 01604 686327.

BRIGSTOCK
Opened in 1985, and formerly a quarry. Traces of old sand pits and diverse habitats, ponds and path loop through Fermyn Forest. Visitor Centre, car park and toilets for the disabled. South of Brigstock village, off the A6116 bypass Thrapston to Corby.
Tel: 01536 373625.

BRIXWORTH
Commands exceptional views over Pitsford Water. Opened in 1990. On-going tree planting and landscaping. Migrating birds come to forage and breed en route for other climes. Summer feathered visitors abound, such as skylarks, and the reservoir attracts a mass of waterbirds and warblers in the scrub. Just off the

A508 Northampton to Market Harborough road at roundabout near Brixworth, by minor slip road serving the Sailing Club. Visitor Centre and toilets with easy access for disabled. Tel: 01604 882322.

IRCHESTER

The aftermath of extensive iron ore extraction, also limestone. The abandoned quarry, now colonised, has become an important feature of this park of 220 acres (81 hectares). Mainly conifers and some hardwoods. Opened in 1971, and sited on the B570 Gypsy Lane in Irchester, turning off the A509 south east of Wellingborough. Visitor Centre, nature trail for the blind and suitable toilets. Tel: 01933 276866.

SYWELL

Prime feature here is the reservoir of 68 acres (28 hectares) and 143 acres (50 hectares) of parkland. On the A4500 (to Northampton), turn at the Earls Barton crossroads towards Mears Ashby. In half a mile, turn into Washbrook Lane to park gates at bottom of hill.Attractive arboretum and an early washpit (near main gate) used by the local community to clean sheep prior to shearing. Obsolete filterbeds now converted to children's playground, butterfly garden and pond-dipping (with boardwalk for disabled).

Access to these, plus angling, hide and facilities for disabled. Perimeter walk around the reservoir 2^{1}/$_2$ miles (4km). Visitor Centre. Tel: 01604 810970.

DAVENTRY

Agreement between Daventry District Council and British Waterways resulted in this area becoming a country park, where the reservoir takes up more than half of the 130 acre (53 hectare) site. On the B4036 Daventry to Market Harborough road one mile east of Daventry. There are hides for birdwatchers, an adventure playground and toilets for the disabled. Information Centre. Tel: 01327 77193.

EAST CARLTON

Owned by Corby Borough Council and opened in 1983, this 100 acre (40.5 hectares) park slopes to a magnificent panorama over the Welland Valley. Turn off the A427 Corby to Market Harborough road. Vast stretches of grassland, ponds, deciduous trees and a striking Hall are within its boundaries. The Heritage Centre, in the converted coach-house, has a band of craftsmen displaying their wares. On the lower floor is a cafeteria with many examples of equipment formerly used in the steel industry on the forecourt. Play places, a static real steam train and other facilities all available to disabled people.
Tel: 01536 770977.

Other Opportunities and Alternatives

Only one of the walks in this book touches on a country park, as readers may be already familiar with them as convenient places for ambles and rambles. There are a number of these, of varying sizes, in Northamptonshire, providing ample space for leisure and pleasure amidst contrasting landscapes, all with free admission.

Of these, to date, six are owned and managed by Northamptonshire County Council, one by Corby Borough Council and one by Daventry District Council. There is a Countryside Ranger in charge of each, and most have a Visitor Centre stocking a comprehensive range of leaflets and information. Many activities take place during the year, including the popular Guided Walks, some embracing a particular theme or slanted toward a certain group, such as senior citizens or handicapped visitors.

Talks, play schemes and events like kite-flying or boules may be organised in the parks, or the locations may be used as focal points for charity runs etc. Such events are usually advertised in the local press.

Another excellent venue, and well worth a trip to our county town, is the Countryside Centre where spacious premises offer changing exhibits of every kind, including conservation issues and volunteer programmes. In fact, everything you have always wanted to know about the countryside but did not know where to seek the answer. Hand-crafted goods, books, tapes of birdsong and much much more, are for sale and it is a source of unique gifts for that 'special' person.

Pocket Parks offer no facilities for the public, but are areas of open access in and around villages, or sometimes urban sites, often rescued from utter dereliction. They may have been tiny, abandoned glades where unsightly rubbish had been carelessly tipped, or simply neglected patches that had become ugly eyesores.

Not only are these precious places havens and habitats essential to our often dwindling wildlife, they also create a local amenity for those who may be unable to travel further afield. Parish Councils seeking advice on this enterprising scheme should contact the NCC Pocket Parks Officer, who will point the way to a package of assistance.

Nature Reserves, growing in number both under the auspices of the NCC and The Wildlife Trust, offer yet another useful opportunity for walkers and nature lovers. Many sites have bird hides for observation, some specifically designed for disabled access.

The Wildlife Trust, in particular, as the name implies, has acquired large tracts of land and water, not forgetting the important SSSIs (Sites of Special Scientific Interest). Some will be noted for certain aspects of nature, such as the preservation of a flora species, or perhaps as selected nesting-sites for birds, whether or not protected. For instance, specific areas are identified where attention is needed to encourage the previously diminishing population of dormice, usually only found in pollarded woodland. Nesting-boxes to accommodate these tiny mammals are being sensitively installed, as these creatures seldom come down to ground level. Odd branches may be tied together over a pathway through the trees so as to make a linking runway over patchy and dangerous spots.

Please remember, wherever you are, respect the countryside and keep dogs under control. Problems regarding rights of way should be reported to the Rights of Way Officer pertinent to the locality.

Two books by the same author, *Northamptonshire Rambles* (1991) and *Exploring the Nene Way* (1992), are to be found in the Countryside Centre and any good bookshop. Both are handy pocket size, offering suggestions for longer walks with details of historical places of interest en route. Circuits in these vary from three to nine miles, and the latter title includes details of the long-distance footpath, the Nene Way, of about 70 miles, with 16 optional loops.

Cherish your countryside!

Other Useful Contacts

Countryside Centre, 9 Guildhall Road, Northampton, NN1 1DP. Tel: 01604 237220.

Pocket Parks Officer, P.O.Box 221, John Dryden House, 8-10 The Lakes, Northampton NN4 7DE. Tel: 01604 237222.

Principal Rights of Way Officer, Planning and Transportation, John Dryden House, 8-10 The Lakes, Northampton NN4 7DE

The Wildlife Trust for Beds, Cambs and Northants, Lings House, Billing Lings, Northampton NN3 4BE. Tel: 01604 405285.